SHOULD YOU BELIEVE IN GOD?

SHOULD YOU BELIEVE IN GOD?

K. SCOTT OLIPHINT

WESTMINSTER SEMINARY PRESS

PHILADELPHIA, PENNSYLVANIA

P&R PUBLISHING
P.O. BOX 817 • PHILLIPSBURG • NEW JERSEY 08865-0817

Westminster Seminary Press, LLC, a Pennsylvania Limited Liability Company, is a wholly owned subsidiary of Westminster Theological Seminary.

This work is a co-publication between P&R Publishing and Westminster Seminary Press, LLC.

Scripture quotations are from *ESV Bible* ® (*The Holy Bible, English Standard Version* ®). Copyright © 2001 by Crossway Bibles, a publishing ministry of Good News Publishers. Used by permission. All rights reserved.

Italics within Scripture quotations indicate emphasis added.

ISBN: 978-1-59638-677-8 (pbk)

Printed in the United States of America

Library of Congress Cataloging-in-Publication Data

Oliphint, K. Scott, 1955-
  Should you believe in god? / K. Scott Oliphint. -- First edition
      pages cm. -- (Christian answers to hard questions)
  Includes bibliographical references.
  ISBN 978-1-59638-677-8 (pbk.)
  1. Apologetics. I. Title.
  BT1103.O465 2013
  239--dc23
                            2013010223

WHAT FOLLOWS is a fictional conversation between a Christian and an unbeliever who offers certain intellectual challenges to the gospel. The conversation is intended to be an *apologetic* conversation—a conversation that includes a presentation of the gospel, but that also answers some of the difficult objections that might be lodged against Christianity. It is, therefore, an attempt to set forth the truth of the gospel in the face of (some of the) intellectual objections that have been given against it. For that reason, the *way* or *mode* of commending the gospel herein is more complex than it might otherwise be, since it is given in the context of those challenges, and by way of a *defense* of Christianity.

I appreciate the opportunity you have given me to speak to you about my own beliefs. You have done this, you say, because you have always been curious about what people believe and why. As you are aware, I am a Christian. But why, you ask, would a particular belief system like Christianity appeal to me, and what exactly does it mean to be a Christian?

I should say at the beginning that this question will be the most important question you will ask in your entire lifetime. If you have any designs on moving from one who is curious to one who is committed, this will be the time. It might not, in God's good providence, be the only time for such a change. But for all we know, it might be. Since neither of us knows the details of our future, we can only say for sure that *this* is the time for you to seriously contemplate such a change.

But why would you want to change at all? You say that your penchant for curiosity has produced little more than confusion.

You recognize that something has to be true. You are not content simply to gather various "truths" from others. You would like to stand on some truth as you inquire of others. This is all very good. As you have said, however, you can't see that you have a place to stand at all. Being curious has only brought a plethora of options that others have chosen. It has done nothing but provide more information to you, and none of the options, thus far, has enticed you.

Your desire for truth is a good one. If you had said to me that truth was not important, or that truth was unattainable, then I might have turned our conversation in a different direction. I might have asked you, for example, if it was true that truth was unattainable. But because you believe that there is truth and you're interested in discovering it, you will likely be interested in what I have to say to you.

If you would allow me to state my conclusion at the beginning of our conversation, I would like you to consider this: The only option available to you that will quell your constant curiosity and give you a place to stand is the Christian option. Every other option you have heard about, or will hear about, will not do for you what you desire. Unless you submit yourself to the Lord Jesus Christ, and stand on his Word, you will never find a real place to stand, or a real place to rest, and your curious search will never end. It is not new or more information you need; it never was. What you need is what I and all other people need—to place ourselves, our trust, our very lives in the hands of the Son of God who came, who lived a perfect life and who died, whose death covered over the sins of many, who was raised from the dead, and whose life is ours when we believe *into* him. What you need, in other words, is to let go of your own hold on life, to repent of your rejection of God, and to trust Christ.

I know you may think that what I have just espoused is the height of arrogance. Not only have I claimed to have possession of *the* truth, but I have claimed that anyone else—past, present, or future—who does not believe as I do will have no claim on the truth. You think, perhaps, that I am claiming omniscience for myself. You think that I know all options available to all men in any and all ages such that no other option will do but Christianity. You think (and you have likely heard this from others) that I am claiming to know the full range of all that is possible. I have just stated that it is impossible to find, believe, and know the truth apart from Jesus Christ. This surely assumes, you contend, that I know all that is possible or impossible.

Does this simply confirm what you have heard about Christians? Is it a clear indication to you that Christians claim to have a monopoly on the truth? Perhaps my belief in God is nothing more than belief in myself, you think, since I seem to claim omniscience; perhaps Christian belief is nothing more than self-confidence *in excelsis*! We Christians, so it is said, claim to know all, and claim to have the only truth. This is the opposite of your own curious quest for truth; it is offensive to you in the extreme.

And how can it be, you ask, that so many brilliant men have been so terribly wrong through the centuries? Am I claiming to be smarter than they? Am I so much more intelligent than the myriad philosophers and scientists of history that I can sweep away all their erudition in the name of my own personal belief system? Is this, too, not the epitome of pride and boasting?

It would have been a shorter conversation if we could have agreed together that submission to Christ is our only hope. But your curiosity has come to the fore again, and it is incumbent on me to try to address your questions.

Let's begin by comparing notes on our past. Because you have discussed so many options with various other friends of yours, you are initially inclined to believe that each of our beliefs, and systems of belief, is mainly a product of our context. Many of those you have talked to, many of the authors you have read and studied, believe what they do because they—through their parents, their education, their surroundings, or a combination of these—have been conditioned to do so.

There can be no question that these contextual factors are a significant part of what we believe and why. My parents, like yours, taught me a multitude of things as I was growing up. They, in effect, chose the environment and context for me. They chose where I would live, where I would go to school, even, in some cases, who my friends would be. So it was for you as well.

Does this mean that what you and I believe is simply a product of our upbringing and environment? Perhaps you've read Joseph LeDoux's *The Synaptic Self* and you agree that we are all products of "nature and nurture." If so, then your own study and questions to others about their beliefs is nothing more than a mere historical quest. Your questions and probing about why certain people believe certain things is a study in contextual anthropology; it has nothing to do with truth at all, and has everything to do with the "accident of birth."

But this constant questioning of others' views has not satisfied you. You have recognized that if we are all simply products of our environments and contexts, then the notion of truth is an artificial one. The best we have, in such cases, are a multitude of autobiographies, none of which tells us anything about "the world" or about "the truth." They tell us only about "this person's world" and "this person's truth." You have learned enough to know that such a view is not practical; it cannot be lived out. It could not provide the foundation for living in this world day to day, or for a family, or a government, or even a meaningful conversation with a neighbor. This is, I think, one of the reasons that you hope to move from curiosity to commitment.

Not only is the "context" notion of truth untenable and impractical, but it is unable to explain what it purports to explain. I was raised in a very religious home. I was sent to religious schools when I was young and was required to be in church every Sunday. This might seem to explain to you why I am a "religious" person now, but it really will not. By the time I was a teenager, I began to recognize many of the problems inherent in the religion in which I was raised. I did not recognize, in any deep and theoretical way, the doctrinal problems of this religion, though they were there. What I did recognize was the emptiness of that religion. I was told to do what I was supposed to do because the church required it. I was told that the church decided what was right and wrong. But then the church officials who would teach me in school could not agree. One would tell us that something was wrong and forbidden, but another, the next school year, would tell us that the same thing was not wrong and could be practiced.

As a man "coming of age," I knew enough to know that such a religion could not be maintained. It depended too much on the latest expert, and it all the while required my firm and undying commitment to its irregular regulations. So I left that religion. I made a decision and announced to my parents that I was no longer a part of that church. For whatever reason, they reluctantly complied. For the next few years, I enjoyed life without constraints. I was free from the shackles of regulations and empty mandates, and I lived like it.

Toward the end of my high school years, I decided to buy a Bible. I had read some Bible stories in my younger days at the religious school, but had never thought of them, nor did I remember most of them. I had never read the Bible for myself, so I decided it

9

was a good time to do that. I went to the local religious bookstore and bought my first Bible. I read that Bible fairly consistently. I began with topics that were listed in the back of it, reading passages that talked about various subjects. I read the Bible for a while until, one day, through a series of circumstances, I was in a meeting where a man was explaining the good news of the gospel. As it turned out, he was describing to me all that I had been reading. The more he spoke, the more I was putting together what I had been reading in the Bible. Somewhere along the way—either when I was reading or when that man was speaking—the Lord changed me. I remember recognizing, for the first time, that what I was committing to was not the religion of my past, but a relationship with the One who had made me and who had redeemed me from my sins.

Well, you say, this simply supports your original idea—truth is contextual. I believe as I do because of my upbringing. The only reason I bought a Bible is that I had been trained to read it at an early age in my religious school. The only reason I was "converted" is that I was going back to my childhood, embracing religion as my parents had taught me.

You, on the other hand, were not trained in this way. The very reason you are such a curious sort, you say, is that your parents sent you to an open-minded school, a school that pushed no religion and that encouraged freedom of thought. Your own parents had gone to such a school (and they turned out to be "good people," as they would remind you on occasion), and it was only right and proper that they should allow you the same freedoms that they themselves had experienced. They believe what they believe because they were given the freedom to do so. So also with you. All of this—my past and yours—only proves the point of the "accident of birth." I believe what I was conditioned to believe, and so do you.

But perhaps because of your curious mind, you yourself have recognized that there has to be more to the truth question than mere conditioning; there has to be more than either context or environment will allow. You recognized this early on when you saw your parents agree on matters that had initially been points of disagreement with them. You recognized that they had to believe many of the same things in order to properly raise you. Your father's "truth" had to congeal with your mother's or there could be no real parenting. You recognized this in a more sophisticated way when you went to the university. Even if your various professors did not agree on central matters (which, of course, given that the university is the temple of freethinking, they did not), you were not able to write one paper defending one kind of truth and another paper, in another class, defending its opposite. You began to see that even if your professors disagreed, you needed to try to bring what you were learning "together." This is what sparked your curiosity, and you've been curious ever since, trying along the way to bring things "together."

Given our respective pasts, we should recognize at least a couple of things. First, the options available to us are either that your life and mine are products of chance or that they were orchestrated by the One who created, sustains, and controls all things. Let's say the former is correct. What that means is that what you believe and what I believe are completely indeterminate. We may want to attach our beliefs, more or less, to our contexts and environments, but even those were a matter of "luck," and so are unable to provide a ground for those beliefs. In other words, you may choose today to believe something that is the opposite of what your parents believe. If you do, that belief has as much "support" as the previous and opposite one. Each belief is simply a matter of what our brains happen to produce at a particular time, and has nothing to do with anything that is consistent, coherent, or rational. These beliefs simply issue forth because they naturally and arbitrarily do, period. The accidents of our births are the first of a multitude of subsequent accidents in our lives. As goes our birth, so go our beliefs. They, too, are accidents. If all that we are and believe is an accident, then we need not continue our conversation. It, too, is an accident and can have no real consequence in the end. What you accidentally believe is different from what I accidentally believe, but such things are no different from the difference in our hair color. They amount to nothing in the end.

The second thing we should recognize is that if our lives were, are, and will be orchestrated by the One who created us, then it is no doubt true that much of what we believe right now has to do with his perfect and exhaustive plan for us and for creation. That plan included who our parents would be, what we would be raised to believe, what our own families would be like, and so on. Because his plan is exhaustive, it includes all things. His plan included the fact that I would decide to buy a Bible and to read it. So as I said above, it is no doubt true that who we are and what we believe has something to do with how we have been "conditioned." But the conditioning that has been behind all that we are and believe is the very same conditioning that is behind this discussion we are having. That you and I are discussing these all-important matters is no accident. It comes to us as a part of God's own comprehensive plan, and it has its meaning and significance only in light of that plan. The difference, then, between your kind of "conditioning" and mine is that yours is accidental, having no reference point, no controls, no purpose, and thus no meaning. The conditioning of which I speak is the polar opposite of yours. It has its reference in the God who made us both; it is controlled by him and his Word, and its purpose, in the end, is to bring glory to him. In other words, God, not chance, is the "All-Conditioner."

You are surely thinking by this point that I have backed myself into an intellectual and logical corner out of which there is no escape. You may think that I am completely unfamiliar with the arguments of philosophy that "prove" the impossibility of a God who controls "whatsoever comes to pass." This kind of God must surely be independent of his creation, while at the same time planning and controlling all that takes place in time. Such a thing is unreasonable; it goes against our laws of thinking and violates what we all take to be true about ourselves and the world.

Let me first assure you that the arguments of philosophers who seek to "prove" that there is no God have not escaped my notice. These arguments certainly do "prove" that God does not exist. Yet they do so not because they really demonstrate what is true, but rather because the arguments begin with that very assumption. Once they start down the yellow brick road of atheism, they are bound to conclude with it. For example, you may have read Michael Martin's proof for the nonexistence of God. In one part of Martin's "proof," he says:

> Consider logic. Logic presupposes that its principles are necessarily true. However, according to . . . Christianity . . . , God created everything, including logic; or at least everything, including logic, is dependent on God. But if something is created by or is dependent on God, it is not necessary—it is contingent on God. And if principles of logic are contingent on God, they are not logically necessary. Moreover, if principles of logic are contingent on God, God could change them. Thus, God could make the law of non-contradiction false; in other words, God could arrange matters so that a proposition and its negation were true at the same time. But this is absurd. How could God arrange matters so that New Zealand is south of China and that

New Zealand is not south of it? So, one must conclude that logic is not dependent on God, and, insofar as the Christian world view assumes that logic is so dependent, it is false.[1]

Examples like this could be almost endlessly multiplied, as I am sure you know, but this one will suffice for the moment.

Notice what Martin is assuming in this "proof." He begins by describing logic as something that has principles that are necessarily true. What he means by this is that logic's principles are *absolutely* necessary; that is, they are necessary just because of what they *are*. Their necessity cannot be dependent on anything at all. To be so dependent, would mean they lose their necessity. So, he says, "if principles of logic are contingent on God, they are not logically necessary." This can only mean that, for Martin, logical principles, defined as necessary, *cannot* be dependent on God in any way, shape or form.

Can you see how this definition of logic *automatically* excludes the possibility of the existence of the Christian God at the outset? Because Christianity has always held that only *God* is absolutely necessary—that is, he is who he is, and is dependent on nothing to be who he is—once logic is thought to be absolutely necessary there is no longer room for an absolutely necessary and self-sufficient God. Martin's logic *takes the place of God*, it does not prove his nonexistence.

Think of it this way. Christianity teaches: "In the beginning, God . . ." (Gen. 1:1). Included in that phrase is the truth that before anything was ever created, there was only the triune God. God has always existed, even before anything else did. He alone has existence in and of himself; everything else has existence only because he freely chose to give it. Since he alone has always existed and has existence in and of himself, *he alone* is absolutely necessary. His existence is not in any way defined or determined by anything outside of himself—not by logic, not by laws, or numbers, or concepts, or contexts, or any other thing. So what Martin holds to be true for logic is actually true only for the triune God. Martin's argument, however, puts principles of logic in place of God; the true God is therefore disallowed entrance into the argument at the outset.

Martin's assertion that "if something is created by or is dependent on God, it is not necessary" itself presupposes that God does not exist. The Christian faith has always held that there are, and must be, two kinds of necessity. There is the necessity that belongs to God alone—a necessity that is alone absolute, the kind of necessity that Martin thinks logic has. And there is a necessity that is what it is because God has created it that way. For example, a square is what it is by virtue of God's creation. Before creation, there was no such thing as a square. A square presupposes relationships of lines and angles, of proportion and numbers. Before creation, there were no such relationships. So also with logic. Logic says that "A is not non-A." But what was this logic before creation? What would represent A when there was nothing but God? Maybe you would say that before creation, "A is not non-A" could be identified as "God is not non-God." The problem with this, however, is that such a statement would mean that God was, at least in part, *determined* by what he was not. In that case, he could not be absolute, or absolutely necessary. He would have to be who he is by virtue, in part, of something he was not. Before creation, though, there *was* nothing that could represent non-A. There was only God. So logic itself is dependent on God's creative activity to be what it is.

The existence of something both created and necessary, like a square, does not mean, as Martin seems to think, that because it is dependent on God it is changeable, once it exists. How could Martin think this must be the case? Only if he derives his notion of God from something other than what

God has said about himself. That kind of knowledge, however, is as arbitrary as it is misguided. God is faithful to himself and to his character. That faithfulness includes the fact that, once determined by God, some things will not change. They are therefore necessary, but only because God has made them the way they are and determined they would be necessary. So the notion of necessity cannot be the same for God and for creation. Any necessity that obtains in creation does so because of God's prior determination. It is, in that sense, a *conditional* necessity, because it is necessary only on condition that God create it, and create it as necessary.

This discussion brings me to your earlier question. You remember that you asked how it could be that so many brilliant men over the centuries could be so terribly wrong. Am I, you ask, claiming to be smarter than them all? I would not want to claim such a thing. I have read and appreciated the brilliance of so many of those who have sought to find a coherent set of beliefs and ideas. I have admired the genius of men such as Plato and Aristotle, Descartes and Kant.

The problem with all these brilliant thinkers, however, is not their brilliance. Their intellectual acumen is obvious for all who want to see it. In many cases, they have provided insights on aspects of the world and its character that can be quite useful. No, the problem is that they have insisted on doing their work, of seeking wisdom, without first deferring to and depending on God and what he has said. They have, in other words, begun their work with the idea that they were able, in and of themselves, to find the solutions to the problems posed. They have asked questions about the nature of ultimate reality, of knowledge, and of ethics, and have sought the answers to those questions within themselves. Beginning in this way is fraught with deep and serious dangers—dangers that guarantee that their genius will turn to vanity and striving after the wind.

Let's see if we can summarize the central dangers that surround such approaches. They are often linked together such that one implies the other, but they are also dangers in their own right. The first danger is the assumption of neutrality. In virtually all the discussions that abound in philosophy and science is the notion that we ourselves and the world around us are "neutral" with respect to God. That is, a supposedly "neutral" and "honest" approach to philosophy, for example, will begin by neither affirming nor denying that the true God exists, but will simply approach the problem by way of the "evidence." "On the major questions of existence and of knowledge," says the enlightened philosopher, "let us see what the evidence is and where it might take us." So, for example, David Hume, the Scottish empiricist, begins his philosophizing by looking at the world around him in a supposedly neutral way in order to see just what it is that we can know. Hume concluded that the only things we are allowed to know or believe are those things that can be confirmed by our own sense impressions. Any idea we might have of something that is beyond the senses is nothing short of fanciful. As Hume put it:

> If we take in our hand any volume; of divinity or school metaphysics, for instance; let us ask, Does it contain any abstract reasoning concerning quantity or number? No. Does it contain any experimental reasoning concerning matter of fact and existence? No. Commit it then to the flames: For it can contain nothing but sophistry and illusion.[2]

In other words, any beliefs we might hold that have their source in something other than "experimental reasoning" (which is to say, things available to the senses) are nothing but "sophistry and illusion." They are meaningless.

You and I would both affirm, of course, that we can glean knowledge from those things that we experience in the world. But that is not Hume's point. His point is that we are *allowed* to believe only those things that we come to understand by our senses (although he does allow for certain basic, "abstract" truths of mathematics). But has Hume really begun his *Enquiry* from a neutral starting point? Is his method really one of letting the evidence speak for itself?

Maybe an example will serve to illustrate my negative answer to these questions. In a recent poll, it was determined that 75 percent of Egyptians do not believe that Arabs carried out the attacks on the United States on September 11, 2001.[3] How could three-fourths of a country's population, in the face of overwhelming and worldwide evidence, believe something so contrary to that evidence? You may say to me that such contrary beliefs are obviously motivated by a certain religious zeal. The only way to avoid an avalanche of evidence such as this is by way of a religious commitment that refuses to see what is plainly there.

This is exactly the point. Hume begins his philosophic investigation with the notion that the evidences do not, in fact, say anything about, or from, the true God. He begins by assuming that the facts themselves are neutral with respect to God. The meaning of those facts must be determined by man himself—in this case by Hume himself—if they are going to "say" anything at all. To assume neutrality at the outset is to assume that God has not spoken clearly through the things he has made. So Hume begins by interpreting facts as *not* created; he begins by supposing that he himself is *not* God's creature and that he is not accountable to God for the way in which he understands those facts. This is surely a bias of extreme proportions; Hume is blinded by his own religious zeal, a zeal that will not see the obvious, a zeal that is certain and resolute about the notion that man (in this case, Hume) is the measure of all things. Not only so, but Hume's bias is a *universal* bias, in that he assumes this neutrality about *all* facts, including the fact of his own existence. As we saw with Martin, once he begins his thinking with this universal notion, he will inevitably end his enquiry in the same way. If it is the case that God has not spoken *anywhere*, how could it be possible for Hume to conclude that God has spoken at all? Surely this is a blind, religious zeal. It is not argued, neither is it proved. It is simply assumed, and assumed in the face of the obvious revelation of God in all of creation (see Rom. 1:18ff.).

This problem, as you can likely see, is inextricably tied to the next one. Not only do these erudite and capable thinkers begin their enquiries by assuming that all facts are *neutral*, they also begin by assuming that their own thinking is itself *normal*. That is, they do not ask, at the outset of their investigation, whether or not their own reasoning and their own method of inquiry is in any significant way *damaged*. Perhaps they assume that they are normal because "everyone" seems to reason in the same basic way. Perhaps they assume it because they cannot imagine that their own abilities could be, as a matter of fact, *dis*abilities. They are like one-eyed men in a land of one-eyed men; they think the entire world is, and could only be, one-eyed.

The problem with this assumption is that it is just that—an assumption. How, we might ask, could one begin to show that one's reasoning and experience were fraught with *dis*abilities? Wouldn't such a demonstration require that one transcend those very disabilities in order to evaluate them?

One way to evaluate the competence of our reasoning and experience is to look at what such methods have produced. It does not take a keen historian or an acute intellect to recognize that the best of our reasoning and experiential methods have yet to produce anything that is definitive, foundational, or useful. A quick glance at the history of thought will show that one thinker's failure is another one's starting point. All the while, the thinking world waits for something on which to stand.

The Christian position maintains that there is something deeply and radically flawed in all of us. As creatures created in God's image, we have violated his law and have sought to detach ourselves from him. This, of course, is not how things ought to be. They ought to be such that we seek, first of all, to please and fear him. We ought to begin our searching, our research, our reasoning, and our demonstration with the fact of who he is and what he has done. Instead, while we remain in our sins, we push him as far as we possibly can from our thinking, our reasoning, our methods of inquiry; we refuse to have him in our thoughts.

This surely means that, in and of ourselves, we begin our inquiries in an *ab*normal way and not in a normal way. The transcendent perspective that we need to discover this abnormality is God's own Word to us. We need an evaluation of our own abilities and disabilities that itself does not depend on ourselves. This evaluation can be had only because God has spoken, and he has spoken in and to our abnormal condition. He alone can make the abnormal normal again. Short of that normalcy, there will be no progress in reasoning, in thinking, in methods of inquiry. All such endeavors, apart from his intervention and our submission, will be stuck in quicksand; they will sink down into nothingness.

If it is the case that neutrality and normalcy are assumed, then it is also invariably the case that naturalism, in one form or another, is also assumed. By *naturalism* I mean a supposition that "the natural" is all that there is. It does not matter here just exactly what is meant by "the natural" just so long as it excludes anything supernatural. Even if "the natural" includes aliens, they themselves are nevertheless known by "natural" means.

The consequences of this naturalism, however, are dire. If "the natural" is all that there is, then what you and I are doing right now is nothing more than what our stomachs are doing as they digest food, or what our hearts are doing as they pump the blood. Our conversation is no different from the natural function of the lion that seeks its prey, or the bird that lays its eggs. What we are discussing right now is as natural as the seasons. They are all a part of the way the world turns.

You will no doubt be aware that such a view destroys any real notion of meaning or of dignity; it destroys any idea of what humans call *love*. It cannot account for the idea of *respect* or of *kindness*. The lion does not respect its prey; the bird does not lay its eggs out of kindness. All that happens is only and simply natural.

But many philosophers have rightly not been content with such a view. The great Enlightenment philosopher Immanuel Kant tried to reconcile the "starry heavens above" with the "moral law within." He knew that the moral could not simply be a part of the natural or the moral would cease to exist. Like most others, he failed to provide a real solution to the problem, but he saw the problem for what it was.

This idea of "the natural," as we can now see, automatically excludes the idea that God is who he says he is, and that he has spoken. It disallows any notion that the triune God is alone absolute (or, as theologians say, *a se*, meaning "of or from himself") and that he has condescended to create, to control his creation, and to redeem a people for himself, all to his own glory. To exclude such an idea is to consign all that we count to be human to nothing more than instinct; it is to destroy all that we take to be meaningful, including this very conversation.

Only by assuming, and affirming at the outset, the Christian God who has spoken can we escape this morass of meaninglessness and despair. Only when we see "the natural" as a product and environment of the supernatural triune God will we be able to give an adequate and satisfactory account of our own lives, of the people we know and love, of the reality of the world, and of the meaning of this discussion that we are having.

But even if you grant that neutrality, normalcy, and naturalism are inadequate foundations for human life and thought, you may still contend that the God of whom I speak, who alone is *a se*, cannot relate himself to you, to me, and to this world without turning into the opposite of what he is. Aristotle's "thought thinking itself" is the only reasonable option if this God is to be and remain absolute.

At this point we reach the crux of all that I have thus far said to you. It was impossible for Aristotle's "thought thinking itself" to relate to anything else without thereby becoming dependent on that to which he relates. If he thought anything other than himself, then he could not be absolute, because his thought would depend on something other than himself.

But if we remember that what is possible and what is impossible is determined by God himself, and not by some abstract notion, say, of necessity, then we can see just why it is that you and I must depend, first of all, on what God has said. It would certainly be the case that an absolute "thought thinking itself" could not be absolute if it "thought" something other than itself; it would depend on that "other" to think. But the triune God of whom I speak is personal; he is not an abstraction, nor is he a collection of abstract notions. Because he is personal, he can choose to act or not to act. He has, as a matter of fact, chosen to condescend, and to create the universe. Because we have chosen to violate his character, instead of destroying us all, he has also chosen to redeem a people. And he has chosen to do that by himself condescending, in the person of his Son, to redeem us. This condescension did not entail that he cease to be the absolute, personal God. Indeed, he could not so choose, since he would then be denying himself. So he remains who he is even while he takes to himself a human nature, in order to satisfy the justice that a holy God requires of sinful people. Here, then, is the answer to Aristotle's "thought thinking itself." It is a God—the only true God—who can maintain his absolute independence and who can also take to himself the characteristics that ensure redemption for his people. He has done that in Jesus Christ. This is why I began where we now conclude. Because Christ has come, has died for the sins of his people, and now lives to intercede, you can come to him with the promise of full redemption. This redemption is not simply a narrowly "religious" redemption; it is redemption of all that we are.

Impossible, you say? Only if *possibility* and *impossibility* are defined according to assumptions of neutrality, normalcy, and naturalism. But if they are defined by God, then even though such things may be impossible for man, they are possible for God.

Your responsibility, in light of what we have now discussed, is the same as mine was those many years ago. Your responsibility is to turn from your desperate and unwarranted assumptions—assumptions that can lead only to empty and vain thinking—and to trust the One who created you and who has come to redeem all who will come to him. I cannot force such a decision on you. I cannot make happen what desperately needs to happen in you.

Only God can do that. If you will forsake your idols of independence and place yourself in his hands, this much is certain: *he will redeem you.*

All that I have said to you boils down to this one truth: the reason I believe in God is that without that belief nothing else can make any sense at all—not my life, not yours, not my work, not my thoughts or relationships or activities. Apart from him, everything is empty. I did not see that so clearly when I came to believe in him, but by his grace I see it now. You, too, can see it clearly, if he gives you eyes to see. In the end, therefore, you must come to Christ, to the foot of the cross, and plead his mercy. Nothing short of that will do.

In conclusion

+ What was the purpose of this conversation? What about the circumstances and content of this conversation make it different from other conversations you might have about the gospel?

+ Why is it important that the curious seeker believes truth is attainable? How does this starting point shape the direction of the conversation?

+ What does the seeker need instead of new information? Why is this? How is this proved throughout the conversation?

+ If all people are products of their contexts, what does this mean for the idea of truth? What are some of the practical and logical problems with this belief?

+ The seeker's curiosity is an expression of the seeker's desire to "bring things 'together.'" What life circumstances can show us that truth needs to congeal in some way?

+ If our lives are nothing but meaningless accidents filled with meaningless accidents, what does that mean for the conversation? If our lives are *not* meaningless accidents, what does that indicate about the "conditioning" we experience in life?

✤ What does Michael Martin mean by the "absolute necessity" of logical principles? How does this automatically exclude the existence of the Christian God? What are the two kinds of necessity that Christians believe in?

✤ What is meant by the "assumption of *neutrality*"? What do people who assume neutrality believe about the world? How does this lead to problems?

✤ What is the danger of believing your thinking is *normal*? How does this result in a lack of definitive truth claims throughout history? What is the Christian response?

✤ What is the problem with a *naturalistic* view? What does it do to our understanding of the world?

✤ How does the Christian God transcend the problems of neutrality, normality, and naturalism? Without him, what are we left with? What is the seeker's responsibility in light of this?

NOTES

1. Michael Martin, "Transcendental Argument for the Non Existence of God," *New Zealand Rationalist and Humanist* (Autumn 1996).

2. David Hume, *An Enquiry Concerning Human Understanding* (n.p.: Forgotten Books, 1958), 123.

3. Pew Global Attitudes Project, "Western Tensions Persist, Common Concerns about Islamic Extremism," July 21, 2011.